Christ
Organiser

Community Organising
for Discipleship and Mission

Tim Norwood

RelationalChurch.UK

Christ the Organiser:
Community Organising
for Discipleship and Mission

Printed by Amazon

ISBN: 9798884818057

Published by Relational Church UK, 2024
www.relationalchurch.uk

Contents

Foreward by Alison Webster

I first encountered Community Organising as a mechanism for churches to 'do' social justice in a local and contextual way. This was back in 2018 when I was Deputy Director of Mission (Social Responsibility) for the Diocese of Oxford. It was a precious discovery; something for which I had been searching for over twenty years as a social justice practitioner with the Church of England! It was clear to me that Community Organising was a powerful and 'missing link' in the churches' social action agenda. As Tim explores in this book, much of what churches spend their time doing serves to mitigate the effects of social injustice. Here was a way of challenging the unjust structures that underpin them.

But as I got to know Citizens UK better, and went deeper into the art of organising, I have come to realise that it is so much more than simply a way of 'doing justice'. I have come to appreciate organising as a spiritual practice.

This invaluable introduction to Community Organising by Tim Norwood explores what this means. Because it is at its heart relational, Organising is about connecting with that of God in each and every one of us, and finding connection. It is about encountering the divine in a diverse range of 'others', and exploring what that means for ourselves, as individuals and as members of the Body of Christ. It is about being 'sent out' into the highways and byways and finding people of peace there – partners in God's mission to transform the world; people of all faiths and none, who are passionate about making the world a better place. It is about seeing that those closest to injustice are those who will teach us most about its dynamics, and guide us towards what needs to be done, as leaders. It is about seeing a future where institutions (simply, groupings in which individuals invest to become powerful together) can become reimbued with trust and reliability. Including our churches.

The story of organising is a story of finding our own voices, and joining with the voices of others. It is profoundly spiritual. This book helps us to see how, as clergy and lay people, we can be part of disorganising world and church, and reorganising it to better fulfil the demands of a kin(g)dom of God.

Alison Webster, Mission Theologian in Residence, Citizens UK

1. Introduction: Learning from Organising

After this the Lord appointed seventy-two others and sent them two by two ahead of him to every town and place where he was about to go. He told them, "The harvest is plentiful, but the workers are few. Ask the Lord of the harvest, therefore, to send out workers into his harvest field. Go! I am sending you out like lambs among wolves. Do not take a purse or bag or sandals; and do not greet anyone on the road.

"When you enter a house, first say, 'Peace to this house.' If someone who promotes peace is there, your peace will rest on them; if not, it will return to you. Stay there, eating and drinking whatever they give you, for the worker deserves his wages. Do not move around from house to house.

When you enter a town and are welcomed, eat what is offered to you. Heal the sick who are there and tell them, 'The kingdom of God has come near to you.'

Luke 10.1-9 (NIV)

In 2008 my friend and colleague, Tim Clapton, dropped in for a one-to-one. He had been on a course about *community organising* and wanted to try some of his new tools out on me.

He told me about an organisation called Citizens UK and his hope that we might start a broad-based community alliance in our city. The aim would be to build people up to achieve social change. It sounded like a good idea so I gave him the names of a couple of people who might be interested.

Two years later, we launched a new chapter of Citizens in Milton Keynes with nineteen member institutions. We were given funding to pay our first community organiser and held our founding assembly.

Since then, I have had some of the most amazing and moving experiences of my life as a follower of Jesus. I will always remember the bitter-sweet joy of meeting refugees at an airport, or the thrill of seeing a prime minister change his mind.

More significantly, I have seen people grow as leaders and transform difficult situations. I've seen God at work in people and places where I would never have thought to go...

This short book is an attempt to learn some lessons from community organising from a Christian perspective. It's not a hand-book on broad-based community organising – but it is a reflection on how churches might use organising both within their congregations and beyond.

Community organising has a lot to teach us about social justice, but I think it's also hugely relevant in terms of discipleship, congregational growth, evangelism and leadership. It can give us a useful model for understanding vocation, power, and purpose.

Community organising is a highly developed practice with deep roots and a rich heritage. The core idea is the relatively simple desire to bring diverse groups together so that they can serve the common good.

This was the goal of Saul Alinsky who developed a number of methods and principles in nineteen-thirties America. His book

"Reveille for Radicals" (1946) became a best-selling wake-up call for social change and influenced the civil rights movement in the nineteen-sixties. This was followed by "Rules for Radicals" (1971) which is still widely read today.

Alinsky's ideas led to the creation of number of broad-based community alliances and movements in the US and across the globe. Citizens UK describes itself as "the home of community organising in the UK". As a charity, it has been building powerful local alliances across Britain for over thirty years, in places like London, Birmingham, Leeds, Somerset, Cardiff, Nottingham, Leicester, and Milton Keynes.

The Milton Keynes alliance is now over ten years old and includes a number of local churches. I was privileged to be part of the sponsoring group that launched it and have been involved in the ups and downs that followed.

As an ordained minister, I have thoroughly enjoyed my experiences of community organising. Churches in the UK face a number of challenges in the twenty-first century. We often feel powerless in the face of huge social, political and environmental change. I believe that organising might help us to release potential that is often untapped!

Challenging Culture

Churches have always been influenced by the dominant culture and values of wider society. This is sometimes a deliberate choice, but it's often a more unconscious process of assimilation. The Church absorbs ideas, some of which are positive, but others less so.

In the past, churches have supported slavery, rejected Darwinian evolution and blocked the ministry of women. It often took a while, but leaders, theologians, churches and congregations worked through these issues and came to a new perspective. Positive ideas from the wider world came into dialogue with scripture and tradition. Intelligent debate influenced our thinking and we changed direction in a Godly way.

Sometimes, however, we absorb new ideas without thinking them through. This often happens because certain ideas are so prevalent in the world around us that they are generally assumed to be true. Not all of these ideas are helpful.

We currently live in an age of **polarisation**. Truth is no longer regarded as relative, but absolute. In this bitterly divided culture, it is not enough to believe that you are right, and your opponent is wrong, your "enemy" must be defeated, crushed, cancelled or dismissed. Living with diversity is not easy when people live in virtual silos, unable or unwilling to spend time with each other. There is a new "legalism" in our culture which makes it difficult for contradictory opinions to co-exist.

Jesus, on the other hand, often engaged with people who belonged to rival religious groups – groups with a deep hostility to his own community. He was particularly gentle with Samaritans who were their historic enemies. He saved his anger for those who shared his Jewish faith, but applied harsh and unforgiving legal codes on others.

In this bitterly divided world, I am often struck by the difference between broadcast and relational communication. Our society prizes **broadcast communication** because it reaches more people. We value a Tweet/post that hits a million people far more than a quiet conversation over a cup of coffee. As a culture, we judge communication according to numbers rather than depth. As Christians, we may want to question this assumption.

Jesus, as we shall see, was not afraid to address crowds, but took time to give people focussed attention. He built a movement that would reach out across the globe by talking to individuals and small groups. For some reason, we think we can do things differently...

Churches have also absorbed the beliefs of **managerialism**. We have adopted the dominant idea that professional managers are uniquely placed to solve our problems, using systems of control, accountability and measurement. This has sometimes produced an ecclesiastical culture which is more centralised, and less collaborative.

Managerialism is seductive. It seems to offer a proven short-cut to "solving problems". Managerialism can produce quick results, because leaders who throw energy at a problem often achieve *something*. They can get things moving quickly, often by ignoring opposition or negative feedback. Managerialism produces quick wins but generally doesn't result in deep change or lasting impact.

Community organising, on the other hand, focusses on building relationships, identifying real needs, nurturing vocation and growing leaders. As a genuine alternative to polarisation, broadcast communication and managerialism, it feels more in step with the values and beliefs of the Church. Jesus operated more like a community organiser than a manager. His approach was deeply relational. He was interested in people's inner motivations and the actions that these produced.

Jesus also got angry. He was angry with the Pharisees who tied people in knots with complicated rules; he was angry about the plight of ordinary people; and he was angry that the World wasn't the way God intended for it to be. As Christians, we need to rediscover our own anger at the injustices and imperfections of this world. If we don't feel an appropriate level of anger, we won't be motivated to make a real difference.

We live in a broken world, but Jesus calls us to help him bring change to those who most need it. We have Good News to proclaim and we need to do this through action as well as words. Community organising is a valuable tool which can help us to do this together.

We need more Christian organisers. We need people who will catch this vision and help others to work together more effectively. We need people who will organise for the sake of the Kingdom.

Some people are offended by the language of organising because it can feel a bit too "political" or "confrontational". Like all metaphors, models and analogies, it has both strengths and weaknesses. I hope you will read this book with an open mind, an attitude of curiosity, and a sense of humour.

Learning from Community Organising

Community organising is a tool for bringing people together to serve the common good. As such, it is no different from other tools, like a hammer, a pen or a computer. The value of the tool is determined by the people who use it and what they decide to use it for.

As a Christian, I find it impossible to separate my beliefs and values from my behaviour and actions. The powerful thing about community organising, is that it enables me to work with other people who hold different beliefs – while maintaining my own integrity. Diversity becomes a source of shared power rather than the roots of division.

I have attended many meetings where people from different faiths have talked about the things that are important to them. The encounter becomes deeper and more significant when we then work together on issues that matter for those in greatest need.

Community organising requires us to start with who we are – what we believe about the world – and how this motivates us. What makes it powerful as a methodology, is that it helps us to turn our deep inner yearnings into shared action.

To those of us who belong to churches, organising can be both strangely familiar and deeply challenging. It resonates with the Christian emphasis on positive relationships, the need for change, and a vision for a better world. It also dares us to take these things more seriously - to focus on action that will achieve results

- to help other leaders to grow - to give serious time to other people and their concerns.

There are many books and courses that introduce community organising. In this book, we are going to focus a few core ideas which I think are both powerful and counter cultural.

Outcomes: Institutions, Leaders and Change

The main aim of Community Organising is to bring people together so that they can make a difference. Organisers achieve this by working in three main areas:

1. **Strengthening Institutions:** Community Organisers focus their attention on local community groups – like churches, schools, trade unions, mosques, synagogues and charities. These institutions are often weak or disorganised - in comparison to business or government. The first task of organising is therefore to strengthen our institutions so that they are able to engage with a wider context.

    Organisers spend a lot of time working on relationships. This is usually done through one-to-one meetings and small group work. These meetings are opportunities for people to share what they really care about. The bedrock of organising is the task of building links and helping communities to articulate their own agenda.

2. **Developing Leaders:** In order to make change, we need more leaders – not more people with grandiose titles - but more people who have influence on those around them and are able to make things happen. As many organisers would put it, "Leaders are people with followers".

    Community organisers build other people up through training, mentoring and coaching. The "Iron Rule" of organising is to "never do for others what they can do for themselves". This is easier to say than to achieve, but it's crucial to organising methodology.

Churches have an unfortunate tendency to slip into clericalism. We use the language of "collaborative leadership", "every member ministry" or "consultation", but our actions often demonstrate a more hierarchical or managerial understanding of leadership. The idea that the "Church is the people" is taught in Sunday School but undermined by practice.

Community organising offers an approach to leadership which turns clericalism on its head. If ministers were organisers rather than managers, their role would be to build up the people of God and encourage leadership in others.

3. **Taking Action Together:** Community Organising was developed as a tool for achieving change. It has proven to be an effective way of helping disenfranchised communities stand together and make powerful people take notice.

   Organisers often look for power-holders who can unlock difficult situations. Who are the people who can help or hinder us, and how do we get them to do what we want? Once the power-holders have been identified, leaders can take action to bring about change.

   Sometimes, we ourselves are the people who need to think differently or do something new. We may need to "do an action on ourselves", as some organisers would put it.

Community Organising is a powerful tool, but it has its limitations. It's good for achieving change, but you need other tools if you want to run a charity properly or manage volunteers. On the other hand, the principles and methodology of organising are useful in a wide range of contexts and situations. There are transferable skills which work even if we're not trying to change the *entire* world.

This little book contains a few reflections from someone who has lived and worked in the overlap between Church and community organising. It is not a complete introduction or a handbook. It won't tell you everything you may need to know. My hope is merely that it will help Christian disciples to see that there is something in this tool that will enable them "to proclaim good news to the poor... to set the oppressed free, to proclaim the year of the Lord's favour."[1]

.

---

[1] Luke 4.18-19. The full quote includes a reference to "recovery of sight for the blind" which echoes Old Testament passages about those who are "blind" to what God is doing.

Questions

1. Think of the people in your church who have a positive impact on others. What do they do that makes them stand out?

2. Can you think of any examples of different groups working together? Was this more effective than groups working alone?

3. What groups and communities do you belong to? What do you think they would want to achieve if they could?

4. Are there other groups or communities in your local area? Do you know what problems they face? Do you know what they hope for?

2. People + Power = Getting things done

'Suppose one of you wants to build a tower. Won't you first sit down and estimate the cost to see if you have enough money to complete it? For if you lay the foundation and are not able to finish it, everyone who sees it will ridicule you, saying, "This person began to build and wasn't able to finish."

'Or suppose a king is about to go to war against another king. Won't he first sit down and consider whether he is able with ten thousand men to oppose the one coming against him with twenty thousand? If he is not able, he will send a delegation while the other is still a long way off and will ask for terms of peace. In the same way, those of you who do not give up everything you have cannot be my disciples.'

Luke 14:28-33 (NIV)

Counting the Cost...

If you want to achieve something, whether it be a DIY project or major social change, it is essential that you work out the cost before you set out on the job. You also need to ask yourself if that cost is worth paying...

In the summer of 2019, I built a gazebo in the garden. The gazebo wasn't that expensive by itself, but I discovered that I would also need to lay some decking for it to stand on, which would involve digging a big hole in the garden, which would need to be lined to block weeds, and so on...

The cost went up as I began to think about the extra materials that I would need – and I rapidly became aware of the time this project would take to complete. Fortunately, I was persuaded (by my family) that it would be worth it. In the end, I enjoyed the work and the family gained some extra space for the summer months. It proved invaluable during the COVID pandemic when we were all trying to live and work from the same house.

There are lots of things that we would quite like to do – but probably won't get round to. Many of us would like to write a novel, but we find it hard to give up the valuable sofa time that this might cost us. Many of us would like to see something good happen in our local community, but few of us are willing to put the work in.

The world is full of good ideas, but most of them come to nothing. The main reason for this is simply that the perceived cost outweighs the perceived benefits.

In church life there is often a lot of talk about things that "someone" should deal with. We can be really good at talking about things – but less good at doing them.

There is a cost involved in making things happen, and the biggest cost is usually time. Are we willing to put in the hours involved?

The Art of the Possible

Time is important, but we also need *power*.

Power is the ability to act. It's neither good nor bad, it simply is. Some people have a great deal of power – through their wealth, status or position – but we all have some form of power. The key question is, do we have enough power to achieve the things that we want to do?

Between 2015 and 2020, I worked with a small "Refugees Welcome" group in Milton Keynes. The members of the group did have some power. They had the power to send emails, talk to people and shift some furniture. This might not seem much by itself, but they used their limited power to organise a wider number of much more powerful people – including politicians, local businesses, churches, schools and mosques. This wider group raised significant amounts of money, furnished a dozen houses, and welcomed nearly a hundred refugees into the city.

Did the Refugees Welcome group have enough power to make things happen by themselves? No, they didn't, but they knew people who did.

When many of us think about the word "power" we think in terms of "power over" – the ability to control other people. We should really think in terms of "power with" – the ability to work with other people to achieve things together.

It is easy to fall into the trap of thinking that "power" is something to be grasped and held. Many dictators started out with positive intentions. They genuinely wanted to gain power so they could make good things happen, but the pursuit of power soon became an end in itself – and this ultimately led to corruption and abuse.

In contrast, Jesus shows us a better way to understand power. As Paul puts it in his letter to the Philippians:

In your relationships with one another,
have the same mindset as Christ Jesus:
who, being in very nature God,
did not consider equality with God
something to be used to his own advantage;
rather, he made himself nothing
by taking the very nature of a servant,
being made in human likeness.
And being found in appearance as a man,
he humbled himself

by becoming obedient to death –
even death on a cross!

Philippians 2:5-8 (NIV)

This approach to power is not weak. Jesus challenges injustice and transforms lives. He demonstrates quite astonishing power on many occasions, but chooses to focus his attention on a rag-tag group of disciples. He builds them up and trains them to be the leaders of the future, while allowing himself to be crucified as part of God's plan.

Jesus counts the cost, and builds power with others – for the sake of God's Kingdom. God doesn't ask the same level of sacrifice from most of us, but we could achieve a lot if we would merely be willing to give up a bit of time and share the credit with others.

The Problem of Power

Saul Alinsky, the founding father of Community Organising, told a story about people on the side of a river. They spotted a baby floating downstream. Full of concern, some of them jumped in and rescued the child, but they were shocked to find that more babies were in the water. Before long, they were working hard to pull children to safety.

One of the rescuers turned and began to walk away.

"Where are you going?" the others asked him. "We need your help!"

"I'm going upstream," he replied, "to find out who is throwing the babies in and stop them!"

Churches have often been very good at identifying people in need and finding ways to help them. We spot the babies in the water and naturally want to do something. This is part of our calling – to respond to human need by loving service. We therefore run food banks, homeless shelters and debt advice centres. We have the ability to do this by ourselves.

Churches have generally been less good at stopping the babies being thrown (or falling) into the water in the first place. In terms of the "Five Marks of Mission", we don't spend a lot of time transforming unjust structures or challenging violence.

The reason for this is often that we don't have enough power to make a difference by ourselves. There are other institutions, rules or structures which control the way things are. In many cases, we would need to persuade powerful leaders, governments or businesses to change their minds or do things differently. This is a bit ambitious for most churches.

Christians are often nervous about the very word "power". It simply means "the ability to act" but it has all sorts of negative connotations. We are aware of the way that power corrupts, and we don't want to be accused of meddling in things that are best left to others. Some of us are nervous about imposing our ideas on people who might see things differently...

Building Powerful People

Broad-based community organising, as pioneered by Alinsky, involves bringing a range of diverse communities together to make a difference together. The idea is that a diverse alliance of institutions has more power than a single group. It is hard to ignore people if they represent a range of individuals and groups from different cultures, religious traditions, ages or backgrounds.

The priorities that emerge from a broad-based alliance are often rooted in the real experience of ordinary people, and have been refined through debate and discussion. This means that the call to action has an authority and weight which no individual can muster by themselves.

Broad-based alliances often involve people with a wide variety of faith perspectives, but I think we could see this as a way of seeking the Mind of Christ, or the Common Good. As Christians, we believe that the Spirit of God is at work in all people, so it is only by listening to as many people as possible that we begin to hear what God has to say.

This is often most powerfully felt when someone who is normally ignored or forgotten is given the chance to speak for themselves and tell their own story.

There is something holy that happens when a cleaner stands on a stage and tells a story about their family and the impact of holding down three jobs – particularly when that cleaner is speaking to the prime minister or chief exec whose office they clean. We enter into a place where the voice of God can be heard, and hearts can be transformed.

Power Analysis

If you want to achieve something, it is important to think seriously about power. Can you do it by yourself? If so, great. On most occasions however, you will need to find people who have the power to help you. They might be people you can persuade to work with you, or people who need to change their mind. Who are the people who can help and who are the people who might hinder you? How can you get them on your side – or out of your way?

Once again, I want to emphasise that "power" should not be seen in terms of "dominance", "control" or "violence". Achieving change may require disagreement, tension or conflict, but it isn't necessary to do this by "defeating an enemy" or "crushing opposition".

The ultimate aim of the Gospel is the reconciliation of all things under God – it's about peace. It's not always possible in practice, but we should aim to achieve positive change that is good for everyone. Can we turn our enemy into our friend and triumph together?

One of the most powerful things I have seen in my time with Citizens has been the use of cakes, flowers, biscuits, smiles, applause and thanks. I am convinced that people are far more motivated by gratitude than they are by blame or accusation.

In Milton Keynes, we have an annual Accountability Assembly to which we invite power holders like politicians and business leaders. We have a number of things that we are going to ask them to do, but we also take time to celebrate things that they have already done. We recognise the good things that we have achieved together before asking them to do more.

Getting Things Done

Otto Von Bismark described politics as "The art of the possible". Many of us prefer to complain, make a fuss or argue a point rather than work for real change. We aren't prepared to give time to learn the "art of the possible" and actually get things done. Getting things done requires us to work with others — often people we disagree with. We may need to compromise or look for goals that can be achieved rather than insist on perfection. Many of us would rather complain that nobody cares or listens – while we achieve nothing.

Community organising is a methodology for making real change happen. It requires an investment of time, so that we can build power to get things done. If we are willing to put that time in, we will be astonished by what we can do.

Questions

1. Think about a time when you felt powerful. What did you achieve? Who helped you?
2. Think about a time when you felt powerless. How did this feel? What prevented you from achieving your goals?
3. List some of your big ambitions and dreams. What is preventing you from making them happen? What are the costs?
4. What might God be calling you to do, either individually or as a church?
5. Who has the power to help you? Who might stand in your way? What can you do to get people on your side?

3. Vision and Values: The Kingdom of God

In the beginning was the Word, and the Word was with God, and the Word was God. He was with God in the beginning. Through him all things were made; without him nothing was made that has been made. In him was life, and that life was the light of all mankind. The light shines in the darkness, and the darkness has not overcome it...

The true light that gives light to everyone was coming into the world. He was in the world, and though the world was made through him, the world did not recognize him. He came to that which was his own, but his own did not receive him. Yet to all who did receive him, to those who believed in his name, he gave the right to become children of God—children born not of natural descent, nor of human decision or a husband's will, but born of God.

The Word became flesh and made his dwelling among us. We have seen his glory, the glory of the one and only Son, who came from the Father, full of grace and truth.

John 1.1-5; 9-14 (NIV)

The Big Story

The story of salvation told in the Bible starts at the beginning of creation itself. The writer of Genesis tells us that it all begins with God, who calls the entire universe into being from darkness. Human beings have always been part of a great plan, but we messed things up as a result of our bad choices - driven by pride, envy and greed.

The Bible is the story of how God transforms human brokenness into the Kingdom of Heaven. It begins with the Garden of Eden, and ends with a city where there is no death, dying, tears or sadness.

Christians see the person of Jesus as the focus of God's big plan for creation. Jesus is "God with us" and represents God's willingness to engage with human brokenness and pain rather than simply ignoring the problem or letting us destroy ourselves. The Cross is God's "No!" to everything that is wrong with the World, and the Resurrection is God's "Yes!" to a new creation.

Followers of Jesus are invited to see our own stories as part of this bigger story. We are not random inhabitants of an unpredictable cosmos, but citizens of Heaven with a mission to fulfil. Jesus calls us to follow him, put our trust in him and join him in a project which will only be completed when the Kingdom comes in full.

The Kingdom of God

The phrase "Kingdom of God" is used many times in the New Testament. The "Kingdom of Heaven" is an equivalent term which uses "heaven" as a synonym for God.

The Kingdom of God is an important concept in New Testament theology. It represents everything that comes under the rule of God. It can therefore be found *wherever* God's will is fulfilled. Some people have therefore suggested that it might be better to talk about the "Realm" or "Reign" of God.

In the Gospels the preaching of Jesus is summarised in the words, "Repent, for the Kingdom of heaven is at hand" (Matthew 3:2, 4:17 and Mark 1:15). This is both a proclamation of Good News and a challenge to change.

The Kingdom is present "now" because of what Jesus has already done, but it is also "not yet" because there is still brokenness in the World. The Kingdom will only be realised in full at the end of time when all things are embraced by God's domain.

What's the Problem?

When I was a teenager, I applied to spend a year with a Christian mission agency. As part of the interview process, they asked me, "What's wrong with the world?"

I was, I have to confess, more than slightly pretentious, and trying hard to be "cool". They were looking for the word "sin" but I was becoming uncomfortable with Christian jargon, and wanted to find more contemporary ways of explaining things.

I muttered something about "people not being very nice to each other" so they sent me away with the instruction to spend time in a university Christian Union...

They were right to challenge my too-cool-for-school attitude to Christian theology, but there is a genuine danger that words like "sin" can become shorthand for more complex ideas. This simple word is confused and burdened as a result of unhelpful associations and misunderstandings. For some people "sin" is primarily about sex, while others see it as a matter of private or arbitrary moral codes.

The original concept of "sin" comes from the Biblical idea that we are falling short of the ideal that God has for the World. The story of Adam and Eve provides a helpful way of understanding this...

The story begins with observation. The couple are encouraged to look at the garden where God placed them. They see the tree of knowledge and are challenged to question the things they've been told. "Surely," the snake tells them, "you won't die if you just have one bite. Go on! It must be nice to eat!"

The observation is limited to one point of view – their own. They can only see what might be good for them, and they therefore lose the bigger picture. This self-centred assessment of the situation encourages them to think in selfish ways and their motives begin to change.

"Why not? It can't hurt. Nobody will ever know. Why can't I have some? It's not fair! I want..."

Before long, these dodgy motives result in a dodgy decision, and the act of decision is deeply significant. Choosing to do something destructive is where the story turns from temptation to inner transformation. There is no going back now...

Both Adam and Eve take a bite from the fruit. They have gone from observation, through changing motives and decisions to action.

But there are consequences. In the story, their new knowledge changes the way they behave and the relationships they have - particularly with God. They are forced to leave the garden and face the brokenness that their actions have caused. As they look out on the World that they have created for themselves, the cycle begins again - this time with jealousy and murder...

Which brings us back to the original question, "What's wrong with the World?"

The answer is a combination of individual failings and systemic problems.

We live in a broken world, and this shapes the way we behave. Our perceptions and choices are narrowed by the experiences we have had. It's hard to blame victims of violence for lashing out at those who have hurt them. How can we judge people who turn to crime so they can escape from crippling poverty?

The bad things that happen are often caused by powerful leaders, big institutions and the way other people treat us, but we are all involved in some way and share responsibility. We can't blame the system unless we also acknowledge our own failure to live as God intended.

The problem with the world is that we are all caught up in a vicious spiral of brokenness, bad choices and negative actions, all of which tend to make things worse rather than better. Some people focus on the failings of individuals, while others are concerned with the systems and structures which shape our lives. In truth, "sin" is both. It's a combination of individual actions and systemic problems which tend to cause harm – whether you're talking about everyday rudeness, petty crime or global warming. This is the context in which we all live and work.

What's the Answer?

For Christians, the answer is found in the mission of God. This is focussed on the life, death and resurrection of Jesus.

Through Jesus, God steps into the vicious circle of broken humanity and begins to subvert it. When he encounters people who are ill or suffering, he heals them. When he sees people struggling with difficult choices, he teaches them. When he meets people who have messed up their lives, he forgives them. At each stage of the cycle, he offers an alternative.

The answer from a Christian perspective is the concept of "salvation" which is another of those complex and confusing theological words.

Some people talk about "salvation" as if it were simply a way of getting a ticket to heaven – if you confess your sins, God will let you in.

There is much more to God's plan than this narrow definition might suggest.

I find it helpful to think of "salvation" as an alternative cycle. It begins with an honest look at the World – as we see things through God's eyes. What is God's plan for creation? How does God want us to live? How have we fallen short? How are we responsible? The Old Testament Law helps us to see where we might have failed, while the Holy Spirit brings our inner thoughts into the light. God is actively involved in changing the way we see the world and our place in it.

Seeing things differently can have a deep impact on our motives, but God promises to do more than that. The great promise of the Gospel is that the Holy Spirit will work within us and that the Law will be written on our hearts. The Fruit of the Spirit, Paul tells us, is love, joy, peace, patience, kindness, goodness, faithfulness, gentleness, and self-control (Galatians 5.22-23). These characteristics are generated as we allow God to be at work in our lives...

Every time we make a good decision, or take a positive action, we help move the circle along. God makes this possible through forgiveness, healing and the work of the Spirit. As broken people we are often unable to do the right thing, but God brings transformation by *changing the story*.

The Good News is that we can step from the vicious spiral of sin onto the virtuous circle of salvation - and Jesus is the way in. This alternative cycle could be described as "the Kingdom of Heaven". It's possible to enter the Kingdom in this life — as we wait for its total fulfilment in the age to come...

Playing our Part

The Church has sometimes been described as God's pilgrim people – it's the community of disciples who have chosen to step from one pathway to another. Christians can't claim to be perfect, but we are (in theory at least) trying to live in the salvation circle rather than the sin circle. We could think of Church as the mutual support group for people who are trying to follow Jesus...

Churches also have an active role to play in the mission of God in the World. They act as the Body of Christ by continuing the work that Jesus began.

Many Christian churches and denominations, recognise the Five Marks of Mission as the best description of the work that we are called to do. These are:

1. To proclaim the Good News of the Kingdom
2. To teach, baptise and nurture new believers
3. To respond to human need by loving service
4. To transform unjust structures of society, to challenge violence of every kind and pursue peace and reconciliation
5. To strive to safeguard the integrity of creation, and sustain and renew the life of the earth

Proclaiming the Kingdom is central – it's how the work of Jesus is described in the Gospels. We do this by nurturing new believers, responding in service, challenging injustice and caring for creation. This is how we help the World move from the vicious spiral of sin and brokenness, to the virtuous cycle of salvation and hope.

Organising for Change

Community organising is a way of helping a diverse group of people come together and take action for positive transformation. It usually involves some form of cycle, which could be illustrated as a version of the salvation cycle we've already seen:

This organising cycle often begins with a listening campaign. The aim is to find out what people are concerned about. What is making life difficult? What would they change? What makes them angry? A listening campaign usually involves a lot of one-to-one conversations as people build relationships, listen to each other and begin to work together...

Community organisers often talk about "self-interest" but this doesn't mean "selfish interest". Organisers want to know what people are energised or motivated by. What's in their heart? What are they being called or driven to do?

I like to think of this in terms of a burden or vocation. What has God put on our hearts that we simply *must* respond to?

These things often emerge through a listening campaign. The aim of community organising is to discover shared interests which might lead to transformative action. Are there things that we all care about? What do we all want to change? Is there something that is affecting some people so significantly that we all want to help?

Once a group has identified some shared interests, it can then set priorities and goals. What will people agree to do together that will make a difference? How can people support each other in solving the problems that have been identified?

A Vision for Change

The Kingdom of God is a central concept in Christian discipleship. It enables us to see where we are going and how we might get there.

As a Christian involved in community organising, I have found the Kingdom to be a helpful way of understanding what I am doing and why. In a similar way, community organising has helped me to understand the Kingdom itself in a deeper way.

We don't need to abandon our theology when we engage with organising. Our theology is an essential gift that we bring to our conversations with others. In a diverse alliance it is important to listen to the motivations and beliefs of others, even if we don't share them. We need to talk about our Christian theology, while listening to the beliefs that others hold dear. It helps us to understand them better, and vice versa. We are then able to find common ground in action.

Questions

1. Think about the place where you live. What would you like to change? What makes you angry?
2. Think about your church? What would you like to change? What makes you angry?
3. In what ways are you part of the problem? What could you do differently?
4. If you wanted to achieve change, who might you need to work with or speak to?

4. Leadership: A Tale of Four Vicars

Once upon a time there were four vicars, and they all had a different way of working with other people....

St Agatha's

The Vicar of St Agatha's was a fairly traditional chap. He was brought up in a church where the vicar did everything and looked after everyone. This was the kind of vicar he had always wanted to be!

He made all the decisions – which saved everyone else a lot of bother.

He was always busy doing things. He took all the services, preached all the sermons, visited all the old folk, and took the assembly at the local school every week.

There was only one set of keys for the church, and he had them in his pocket – after all, he was always the first to arrive and the last to leave...

Everything went well until he retired. The Church wardens called up the Bishop and asked who was going to open the church on Sunday...

St Bertha's

The Vicar of St Bertha's ran a tight ship. Before ordination she had been a company secretary and knew how a business should function.

She had a Monday staff meeting, when she gathered the church wardens, organist, cleaners, verger, and other volunteers. She would give them a brief pep talk, and then dish out the instructions for the week.

Everything went like clock-work. She would check up on all of the members of her team during the week and make sure they were on-target and properly supported.

Sunday services were a real team effort with readers, intercessors, Sunday school leaders, a welcome team and worship leaders – and everyone was drilled to perfection!

When she moved on to a bigger church, she left a manual of instructions for people to follow...

St Creosote

The Vicar of St Creosote's was a real people pleaser. He didn't like people to be unhappy so he worked hard every day to keep them from getting cross.

There was a very powerful church council who met every month to make all the big decisions – like what the vicar should be doing.

Every Saturday morning one of the churchwardens would pop in to see the vicar (because it was the vicar's day off and he was bound to be in). He would let the vicar know what extra problems had come up so that they could be dealt with promptly.

The churchwarden thought this was a very supportive thing to do...

One Sunday the vicar didn't turn up in church. He'd packed his bags during the night and fled to a small Scottish island where nobody could find him...

St Dawn's

The Vicar of St Dawn's liked people, and she wanted to treat them as grown-ups. She didn't want to be a one-woman-band, a dictator or a push-over. She wanted to give people responsibility for their own decisions – and help them to grow as disciples.

The church council meetings were always well-attended and fairly lively. She chaired the meetings, and made sure that everyone's voice was heard. There were a lot of arguments and disagreements, but people (usually) made up afterwards.

She was very good at making sure the council didn't make a decision unless there was someone willing to make it happen. They had a number of teams and working groups.

She spent a lot of time thanking people for things that they were doing for God – and she was convinced that God was at work in all people.

When she retired, they carried on regardless. The vicars of St Agatha's and St Bertha's both applied for the job, but the church members weren't sure that either of them was the right fit...

Collaboration: Decisions and Actions

The word "collaboration" means "working together". It's heavily used in church circles, because people generally think it's a good thing. Most clergy job descriptions and adverts use the word somewhere, and very few ministers would say that they are not collaborative.

The problem is that we have a variety of understandings of what collaboration means and how we might work together. All four of the vicars in the story (with one possible exception) thought that they were being collaborative.

The Vicar of St Agatha's was doing everything he could to help people be Christians. If pressed he would say that he was doing *his* bit, so other people could do *theirs*. In reality, he was a one-man-band.

The Vicar of St Bertha's was making all of the decisions herself, but dishing out the jobs. She was a great delegator, and took pride in supporting her people. She was helping people to work with her for the sake of the Church. There is, however, a fine line between good delegation and dictatorship...

The Vicar of St Creosote's (poor man) had surrendered all decision-making power to the people. They were liberated to make decisions – but they thought it was his job to do all the action.

The Vicar of St Dawn's however, was determined that she would share both decision-making and action-taking with the rest of the church. Her job was to facilitate and enable others.

All four vicars had a different understanding of "collaboration" and the differences relate to both decision-making and action-taking. These can be plotted in a simple chart:

The chart maps each vicar according to the way they share or focus decision-making and action-taking. For example, in the case of St Agatha's (A) all of the decisions and actions are focused on the vicar, while at St Bertha's (B) the vicar makes most of the decisions, but shares out the actions...

This is a very handy way of modelling what we might mean by "collaboration". Perhaps you could think about your own church or leadership style? Where would you put yourself or your community on the chart? What is shared and what is focused? How widely shared are decisions and actions in your context?

Activists, Mobilisers, Servants and Organisers

On the whole, an "activist" focuses on what they want to do. They might work with other people, but only when it suits them. The Vicar of St Agatha's (A) is a bit of an activist. Activism has its place. Activists can sometimes get things done – even if the entire world seems to be against them - but it can have its limitations...

The Vicar of St Bertha's (B) is a "Mobiliser". She already knows what needs to be done and sees the purpose of her job as getting other people to make it happen. She focusses on training, supervision and support. This means making the tasks as clear as possible so that everyone can contribute in some way. Mobilising is a great way to get lots of people into action. It's a popular approach for campaigners because "people power" can make a difference.

The Vicar of St Creosote (C) is a "Servant". He's happy (in theory) to serve the interests of a wider group. There is a real need for people who are willing to "service" the needs of teams, groups and communities. Every organization needs people who are happy to muck-in and make things happen. There are always chairs to shift, dishes to wash, minutes to write and accounts to audit. There is a danger, however, that *servanthood* can become *servility*, which is definitely happening in this case...

This book is about "organisers" – people like the Vicar of St Dawn's (D) who want to build communities and leaders. This happens by continuously expanding the number of people who share in decision-making and action-taking. I genuinely think that we need many more organisers in our churches.

Organising has its limitations though. It takes time and requires a lot of effort. There are situations in which it's much more efficient and appropriate to be an activist or a mobiliser – and willing servants are always helpful...

Questions

1. What do you think your "leadership" style has been in the past? Have you operated as an activist, a mobiliser, a servant or an organiser? Has your style changed in different contexts?
2. Do you find it easier to share decisions or actions?
3. What is the default style of leadership in your church?
4. Can you think of occasions or situations where this has been helpful?
5. Are there times when a different approach might have been better?
6. Can you think of an opportunity to involve someone else in a decision or action this week?

5. Relationships: Building Community

"A farmer went out to sow his seed. As he was scattering the seed, some fell along the path, and the birds came and ate it up. Some fell on rocky places, where it did not have much soil. It sprang up quickly, because the soil was shallow. But when the sun came up, the plants were scorched, and they withered because they had no root. Other seed fell among thorns, which grew up and choked the plants. Still other seed fell on good soil, where it produced a crop—a hundred, sixty or thirty times what was sown. Whoever has ears, let them hear."

Matthew 13.3b-9 (NIV)

The Perils of Broadcasting

I once visited a small church which taught me something really important about communication. On the day in question there were only six people in the congregation. At the end of the service, one of them stood up to give the notices – because you simply can't have church without notices!

After the usual messages about future events, she pointed out that there were many gaps on the coffee rota. She told people how important the rota was, and asked them to go home and pray about it – and think seriously about putting their name on the list next week...

I really wanted to say, "Hang on! There are six people in this church – counting me! Why don't we put the kettle on and talk about it? We could fill the gaps in by the time the water boils!"

I didn't do it, but I wish someone had.

This small church was mirroring behaviour from bigger churches. They knew that "proper" churches have notice sheets, newsletters and rotas – and they were determined to make their church look and feel like a "proper" church.

Unfortunately, the "notices" strategy doesn't work all that well in bigger churches either. I've sat in too many church council meetings where we discussed ways of filling rotas or roles. The discussion always ended with a decision to put an article in the news sheet and make an announcement in a service. The results were usually disappointing.

Usually disappointing, but not always. The odds can be in your favour because size matters when it comes to "broadcast" communications.

By "broadcast" I mean any form of communication that comes from a single source and aims to reach as many people as possible. Radio and TV work on this basis. Advertisers are willing to pay serious money to get their message out to millions of people – because they only need a small percentage of responses to make it worthwhile.

Let's say, for example, that you run a company selling soft drinks and you know that one in a hundred people will respond positively to your advert. If your advert reaches a million people, you can be fairly sure that ten thousand people will buy your product. That's a worthwhile rate of return.

If the same proportion applies to church notices, you would need at least a hundred people in the building before you have the chance of getting a single response. The average British Church has a congregation of around forty, so it is quite likely that nobody will respond at all.

The one in a hundred figure is notional, of course, but it's a good rule of thumb. What it helps us to do is understand the potential value and limitations of broadcast communication. Broadcasting has its place – but must not be overused.

The Parable of the Sower describes the problem very nicely. The Good News of Jesus is strewn like seed into a field. Some falls on the path and is eaten, some on rocky soil and dries up, some into bushes and the plants are choked. Only a small proportion of the seed falls on good soil and produces fruit. Jesus understood the problem of "broadcast evangelism" only too well.

The Power of being Relational

The Gospels tell a number of stories where Jesus talks to large crowds, but there are many more stories of smaller encounters – often with only one other person involved.

John's Gospel is dominated by a series of significant one-to-one encounters – Nicodemus, the Samaritan Woman, Mary Magdalene, Simon Peter and so on... Jesus does his most important work in small groups and one-to-ones. The Son of God feels compassion for the crowds because they are like sheep without a shepherd, but he focuses in on individuals who are given more serious attention. He goes after one sheep at a time, rather than ninety-nine in one go.

This is "relational" rather than "broadcast" communication. Jesus takes time to get to know the other person – he asks questions, listens carefully and builds a relationship. This results in deep change and profound action.

Relational communication has strengths and weaknesses. It requires more work to reach fewer people. It can take a lot of time – but every encounter is valuable in some way and the results can be very significant.

Working relationally makes sense in terms of Christian theology, which values each and every human being as a unique child of God. The core of God's mission is reconciliation and wholeness. We participate in this by drawing closer together as individuals and seeking the Common Good together.

44

Christians believe that the Spirit is active in everyone, and that we all have a part to play as disciples. Working relationally is a good way of recognising this fact as we build community rather than merely complete a project.

The quickest way to fill a coffee rota is to ask the whole congregation in one go. It can be done, and sometimes works. The alternative is to speak to people one at a time – or in small groups – perhaps targeting people who stay for coffee and look reasonably friendly. You have a chat about church and what they like about it. You discover that they really value the time of fellowship after the service. You explain that you are responsible for the coffee rota, but filling it in is a bit stressful. They offer to help from time to time. You ask them if they can do every third Sunday. They agree. Job done.

Relational communication is remarkably powerful, enjoyable and very natural, but incredibly counter cultural. We live in an age when people would prefer to tweet their news or post it on Facebook. We are in a rush and feel time-poor so we go for the quick option of broadcasting our messages to as many people as possible. We are left with shallow relationships, busy diaries and empty rotas...

Organising using One-to-Ones

Community organising is the art of bringing people together so they can make a bigger difference in the world. As Christians we root our understanding of change in the cosmic picture of Salvation History. There are huge needs and problems to address – but organisers address them using the tools of relational communication.

Organising is about building power so you can achieve the change you want to see. Organisers bring people together so that they can agree a common agenda and act in unity. The tool that makes this possible is the one-to-one.

I learned a key lesson about one-to-ones when I was a curate. My boss (nice man that he was) asked me to take on the task of re-ordering one of the churches in the parish. This basically meant - moving the chairs.

Anyone who knows anything about churches will know that you should never tinker with chairs or pews – unless you have thick skin or a hard hat. Someone is going to be very cross with you!

The traditional joke comes to mind:

How many Anglicans does it take to change a light bulb?

Response: **Change?!**

I had learned enough about churches by this point to know that a managerial approach would not work. A managerial approach would involve me going away, coming up with a big vision, drawing up a plan and then presenting it to the church council with a PowerPoint presentation. We would put it to a vote and I would have the enjoyable task of making it happen – against the inevitable barrage of objections.

I chose instead to have a series of one-to-ones. I visited each of the key people in turn, and talked to them about the church and what they felt the main issues might be with the building. I listened and we played with some ideas. After each meeting, I tried to capture what I'd learned on a plan which slowly developed.

In a number of cases I went back to people a second time to share what other people had suggested. Bit by bit a re-ordering plan came together.

After a while, I was reasonably satisfied that we had something that captured the ideas that people had come up with. It would give us a decent coffee area, more space for children's work, and a less cliquey seating plan. When I brought the plan to the council, they recognised their own ideas in the document, voted it through and then made it happen.

This is a relatively trivial example of achieving change through one-to-ones, but I think it demonstrates a few key principles:

The most important one is to **Listen!**

It's all too easy to think that we know what problems people face and it's equally easy to come up with solutions that we think will work. It is much more helpful to listen to the people most affected by any issue. They know how it really affects them, and they will also have some ideas about the solutions that might actually work. Unless we listen properly to people, we will miss ideas and possibilities that could transform the world!

Ministers are particularly prone to managerial behaviour. It's really not their fault. The system encourages it and there are many training courses on offer that nurture top-down leadership.

Organising is primarily a bottom-up model. It begins by listening to the people who are most affected by any particular situation and taking them seriously. An organiser doesn't do things "for" or "to" others, but seeks to do things "with" them.

This brings us to the second important principle, and that is about **Alignment.**

We're going to explore this in more detail in chapter six, but it begins to happen in a good one-to-one. People naturally look for common ground, and a relational meeting will often lead to a shared agenda.

In my story about the pews, it's important to note that I shared my self-interest while listening to the self-interest of others. I had been given a task and I was looking to them to help me. They wanted the church to change in particular ways. We looked for ways that we could re-order the church so that it helped *them* achieve something that *they* really wanted. It became *their* plan as much as it was mine.

I also did some work to connect the different people involved. They didn't all want the same thing, but there were compromises that could work for everyone. By the time we took the plan to the church council, it was a *shared* plan which most people had helped create and everyone wanted to make happen. The result was positive change rather than a bad-tempered revolution.

Using Relational Meetings

Working relationally takes time and requires a lot of planning, but its impact goes much deeper and can be incredibly powerful. It's easy to underestimate the significance of one-to-ones, or feel that there are more efficient ways of making things happen. I would suggest, however, that a relational model is worth the effort. It's theologically appropriate, enormously practical, and much more fun!

The danger is that we can easily mistake the things we already do for relational meetings, while the reality is often far off.

Many Christian ministers are faithful visitors, but a cup of coffee and a nice chat is not what we're talking about when it comes to community organising. A one-to-one is not therapy, or a way of showing people that they are valued – it's an intentional conversation which aims to explore individual and shared vocation, and it results in some form of action.

One-to-ones are the most powerful relational tool that we have, but there are others. Some organisers use "house meetings" where small groups gather to share their stories and experiences together.

When I became an Area Dean, I carried out a series of one-to-ones with clergy and lay leaders. I soon became frustrated that I was learning a lot about them, but I needed them to learn about each other. I decided to experiment with what I called "Deanery Lunches" as a way of bringing people together. I found that six was the optimum group size. There were enough people to make useful connections but not so many that we split into two conversations. These slightly larger relational meetings made a real difference in bringing people together, generating ideas and powering change.

There is an art to having good one-to-one conversations, there is also an art in deciding when and how to have them. A planned series of meetings is often called a "listening campaign". This is a programme of relational meetings carried out with a specific focus and target group – usually coordinated by a team who work together.

Christians are generally good at conversation. The average church social or post-service coffee time demonstrates that people can actually be quite friendly. But we're less good, on the whole, at making those conversations focussed and purposeful. Community organising challenges us to use our natural ability to connect as a way to make a bigger difference in the world.

Here are some of the ways that relational meetings could be used by churches:

1. **Growing Disciples:** If you want to nurture disciples in your congregation, the best place to start is through one-to-ones. The vicar, or other leaders, could work their way around the congregation, giving each person some serious attention.

   The aim would be to listen to what each person is feeling. Sensible questions might include:
   - What issues are you concerned about?
   - What do you value about the church?
   - What would you like to be different?
   - What makes you angry?
   - How would you like to contribute?
   - What might you need in order to grow further?
   - What is the next step forward for you?
   - What will you do to make this happen?

   Remember the Iron Rule of organising:
   Never do for others what they can do for themselves!

In other words, the aim would be to help other people grow, not generate a to-do list for yourself. You would need to be really honest about the likely outcome of the meeting.

For example, if they say that the church needs a youth group, don't promise to set one up, but ask them what they would be prepared to do to make it happen. If you can't find anyone who is prepared to take action, then you can safely assume that people aren't really committed to the idea - or it's not the right time yet.

What you can do is bring people together. If you find a number of people who want to start a youth group, then you could call a meeting and see if they could make it happen together...

People who come to church often want to grow as human beings and disciples, but please don't assume that you already know what this might involve. Conversations like this can lead in unexpected directions. Your role is to help the other person articulate what God is calling them to do and then work out how they could turn this sense of vocation into action.

2. **Reaching Out:** Our one-to-ones don't need to stop at the doors of the church. There is no reason why we shouldn't do the same with people outside of the Christian community.

   Many churches have carried out listening campaigns in their local communities which have helped inform their plans and build support for new initiatives.

   People are often happy to help. You could send a team out to ask some of these questions:

   - What do you like about this area?
   - What problems do people face in this community?
   - What would you like to be different?

- If you could change anything what would it be?
- What are you angry about?

As before, don't promise to do anything specific but ask them who they think could help. They might volunteer themselves, or they might give you some new contacts...

Conversations like these often have significant impacts. You will get to know your area better, and build some really positive relationships with people who feel more valued. Some of those people will get involved in projects, and might even join your church. You obviously can't assume that this is going to happen, but a church that cares about things that matter to people can be very attractive.

3. **Changing Something:** There are times when the focus of your one-to-ones needs to be very specific. It could be the coffee rota or the seating plan, or it could be a serious question that needs to be asked.

There have been churches which were on the point of closure and asked a very pointed question: Should we close the building and stop meeting?

An internal "Listening Campaign" would be a good way to involve more people in exploring a problem and getting them to generate solutions.

A team could carry out a series of one-to-ones within the congregation, listening to people and raising questions – much as I did with the re-ordering project.

One of the normal side-effects of a listening campaign like this, is that it generates energy and engagement. Churches that were on the point of closure have been re-energised and new life has emerged.

Never underestimate the power of one-to-ones.

4. **Building an Alliance:** Citizens UK has been building broad-based community alliances across the UK for over thirty years. These alliances have included mosques, synagogues, schools, universities, unions and a large number of churches.

   Churches are often enthusiastic members of Citizens because they know that working with other people is a good thing.

   Building a broad-based alliance takes time and only happens through building relationships. Any Citizens UK community organiser will tell you that you need to do a lot of one-to-ones!

Making it Happen

I've spoken about one-to-ones so many times that some of my friends joke that that they are becoming bored – at least I like to think they're joking. The truth is that I'm increasingly convinced that this is a message we need to hear, but we keep slipping back into old habits.

The Parable of the Sower is very relevant here. The good news is that God has given us a powerful tool that we can use. We know it works, and people enjoy doing it, but it takes time and we're in a hurry.

Sometimes the crows of disbelief come and snatch the idea from our paths – surely the big churches have a better solution – just use X (Twitter), notice sheets and PowerPoint presentations – broadcast your way to Heaven!

Sometimes we get the idea, have a go, but get bored. Like the seed on stony soil we have short-lived enthusiasm, but slip back to our default setting.

Sometimes we're choked by the thorn bushes of opposition as other people do whatever they can to stop us working relationally because they can't see the point.

But sometimes, I meet someone who gets it. They go away and do their one-to-ones and come back astonished by what happened. They have seen barriers fall away, powerful relationships formed and intractable problems shifted. Like the seventy who Jesus sent out with the good news, they come back rejoicing because of what God is doing!

You might think that one-to-ones are old hat, a waste of time or a short-lived fad, but I challenge you to have a go. If you take this way of working seriously, then the results can be astonishing!

Questions

1. When was the last time you had a one-to-one conversation with someone in your church? How did it feel? Did anything come from this?

2. How might you use one-to-ones in your church? Are there any ideas in this chapter that you could use?

3. List three people you would like to have a one-to-one with. Why would these be good people to talk to? What might you ask about?

4. Will you make a commitment to do one or more of those one-to-ones? When will you aim to do it by? If you are doing this in a group, can you hold each other to this?

6. Alignment: Finding Direction

As they were walking along the road, a man said to him, "I will follow you wherever you go."

Jesus replied, "Foxes have dens and birds have nests, but the Son of Man has no place to lay his head."

He said to another man, "Follow me."

But he replied, "Lord, first let me go and bury my father."

Jesus said to him, "Let the dead bury their own dead, but you go and proclaim the kingdom of God."

Still another said, "I will follow you, Lord; but first let me go back and say goodbye to my family."

Jesus replied, "No one who puts a hand to the plow and looks back is fit for service in the kingdom of God."

Luke 9.57-26 (NIV)

Many Visions Make Work Hard

There is a wonderful phrase in the Book of Proverbs, and it often gets quoted when people talk about strategic planning: "Where there is no vision the people perish" (Proverbs 29.18). The implication is that a community needs a strong sense of direction or purpose if it is to flourish or even survive.

Over the years, I have begun to wonder if the problem is often not the lack of vision, but the fact that there are too many.

Churches, like most communities, rarely agree amongst themselves. It is fairly unusual for Christians to speak with one voice. Ask six church members for an opinion and you will get at least six different responses.

This is fine in many ways, and reflects the glorious diversity that God has given to us as the Body of Christ – but it can be deeply problematic when it comes to decision-making...

I remember one small congregation with more visions than it had members. People were pulling in so many different directions that the church ultimately pulled itself apart...

Seeking Alignment

A church is a community of people linked together through a web of relationships. It's possible to illustrate this using a network diagram which describes the way individuals are held together. Here is a simple example:

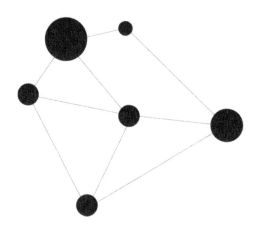

In this example, the dots represent people and the lines represent the relationship between them. The dots vary in size according to the relative influence or power that different people have. The lines indicate relationships which could be measured in terms of time spent together or the frequency of contact.

It's immediately apparent that each person is different in terms of relative power or the number of connections they have. This has an impact on the ability that they have to lead.

Leadership is often defined in terms of influence. It's the ability to influence the thoughts and behaviour of other people. In this simple community, each person could be thought of as both a leader and a follower. They can all influence the people around them.

I like to demonstrate this by drawing arrows, to illustrate the relative influence of each person:

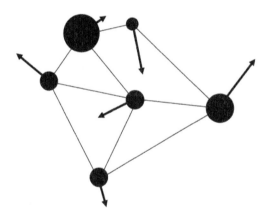

The arrows are pointing in different directions. Each person is pulling in the direction that they believe the group should go. Some arrows are longer or shorter, because people put varying amounts of energy into leadership. Some people are very determined, while others are a bit uncertain. Everyone is part of the community, so everyone has some form of influence on those around them – whether they acknowledge this or not.

The danger is that people are pulling in so many different directions that the group doesn't go anywhere fast. In fact, the different forces can easily cancel each other out so the community doesn't go anywhere at all!

Without a vision the people might perish, but with too many visions they are lost!

The primary task of community organising is to build the relationships between diverse people, so that they can pull in a common direction. It's a proven methodology for making this happen.

The most important tools are relational meetings and assemblies.

We looked at relational meetings in Chapter Five, in particular the one-to-one conversation. One-to-ones are encounters between people which focus on listening, shared-interests and agreed action. They enable two people to come together and discover what they could do to help each other.

Imagine, for a moment, that the six people in our notional community start to have one-to-one conversations with each other.

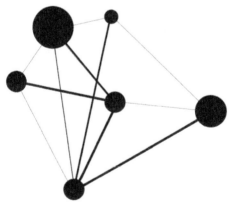

The first thing that would happen would be a strengthening of relationships between people as they get to know each other better. In the diagram this is illustrated by thicker lines between the circles.

There are also more lines, because some members of the group will have spoken to each other for the first time. Everyone is better connected.

They are better connected but not evenly connected. We all get on better with some people than with others. The overall result is nevertheless a strengthening of community ties.

The next thing you would notice is that people will begin to shift in their thinking. As they communicate and share thoughts, they influence each other and begin to change as a result.

It might be imperceptible at first, but the group will begin to develop a shared mind. The more they talk to each other the more they will find common ground.

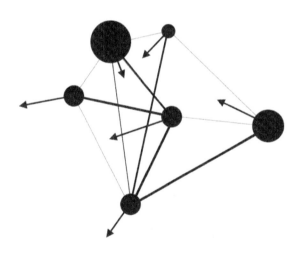

This "alignment" will not be perfect. Some people will continue to pull in their own unique direction, but the various forces acting on the group will begin to come together.

Organising through Assemblies

I love the concept that many denominations have of the Church Meeting which, at least in theory, "seeks the mind of Christ together". I know the reality can sometimes feel less than perfect, but the idea is helpful. As spirit-filled disciples, we listen to what God is saying to us through one another. The aim of the meeting is to discern the will of God together.

In community organising, the equivalent of a Church Meeting is an *assembly*. An assembly is a larger gathering which brings together the member institutions of a community alliance.

There are various forms of assemblies. An "accountability assembly" is a meeting with politicians or other powerholders. It can be a powerful way of demonstrating the diversity and scale of an alliance.

There are also internal assemblies where decisions are made, and priorities set.

In Milton Keynes, as in many Citizens alliances, we ran an annual cycle of larger gatherings. I found these events great fun, but they also revealed the serious challenges involved in working together effectively:

1. **Leaders Forum**: The year would begin with a listening campaign. The idea was that each member institution would reach out to its wider community and bring back any findings to a "leaders forum". In practice, only a few carried out a fully-formed listening campaign, but most groups were able to bring something.

   The "leaders forum" was a gathering of people from different member institutions. The aim of this assembly was to create a list of possible priorities for the alliance. We usually asked each institution to make a short presentation, listing the findings of their listening campaign. We would then try to group the various observations into themes, like poverty, climate change, transport or homelessness.

   We would often end up with a dozen big themes. The next step would be to set up working groups who would refine the themes into more specific plans. We would only move forward with a theme if there were people from three or more institutions who were willing to join the relevant working group.

The working groups would be given a few weeks to think things through and come up with more concrete plans. It was not unusual for some of the working groups to fade away quite quickly, and the number of potential themes would drop from a dozen to as few as four or five...

2. **Delegates Assembly:** A couple of months later, we would come back together for a larger "delegates assembly" where representatives of the different member institutions would vote on which priorities we would take forward.

   The aim was to come up with a shorter list of actions that we could take forward as an alliance. These would include "asks" – which we could present to relevant powerholders.

   This is often where we would lose focus...

   The first danger was the desire to do everything. People didn't like the idea of dropping a potential campaign so we often voted everything through.

   Working groups also tended to come up with too many ideas. This was particularly true for huge issues like climate change. There were so many possible asks and actions, that the group would often produce a long list that might take twenty minutes or more to present.

   These were all good ideas, and the issue was important, but we needed more focus. In trying to do everything, we would often end up achieving nothing.

   We found that it was often better to have more limited goals. For example, the Living Wage group decided to find 50 Living Wage employers before the 50th Anniversary of the Milton Keynes. This was a challenging target to achieve, but it was very Specific, easy to Measure, Achievable, Realistic and Time-bound – or SMART as the acronym goes.

3. **Accountability Assembly:** Our annual cycle reached a crescendo with the "Accountability Assembly". This was the largest event of the year with a serious push for each member institution to bring as many people as possible.

   The aim was to meet local politicians, business leaders and other powerholders who could help us achieve our goals. We might present a list of "asks" to the leader of the council. The Living Wage group would give certificates or cake to companies who had signed up to the Real Living Wage. It was always a great event with lots of energy.

   As with the Delegates Assembly, we found that it was easy to end up with too many campaigns, actions or asks. The more we tried to do, the less we achieved, but good things did happen as a result of those assemblies.

   The Accountability Assembly was not the end of the cycle, of course. The working groups would normally continue to meet and push forward on their agendas.

   The cycle would then begin again. Some campaigns would continue, some would be completed, and others would fade away for lack of interest.

The benefit of this cycle was that it gave us a mechanism for identifying key issues and deciding which ones to focus on. Our assemblies were often very energetic and exciting.

The problem was that we often failed to focus. It was all too tempting to embrace every possible agenda and try to do everything at once.

I therefore won't pretend that our assemblies were perfect. We made lots of mistakes and missed serious opportunities. On the other hand, they did enable us to focus the attention of our member institutions on issues that mattered. We could have done better, but it's really not easy to get people to work together.

Many Hands...

There are three main things that I have learned through these experiences.

Firstly, there is a lot that churches and local community groups can achieve together if they choose to. In Milton Keynes, we were able to achieve a few significant wins that made a real difference to people in our city.

We often feel powerless, but there is a lot we can achieve if we are willing work together.

Secondly, churches and community groups can only do this if they focus on a small number of achievable goals. There are so many things that we could – or should – do, but it is better to focus on a few clear priorities at a time. If you try to do everything at once you will fail, but if you focus on a few important goals, you are more likely to succeed – and can then move on to something else.

As the old proverb says:

You can eat an elephant, if you do it one bite at a time!

As communities, we can't solve all of our problems in one go, so we need to focus our collective energies on one thing at a time.

Thirdly, the work of bringing people together never stops!

This last point is important. People have a habit of losing enthusiasm over time. Teams naturally decline as members move on. Communities get distracted by multiple agendas. A sense of focus rarely lasts.

This means that you need to keep pulling people back together, encouraging conversation, shared vision and focus. You need to keep recruiting new team members, nurturing leaders and developing a sense of common purpose.

If you want to make a difference as a church, or as a community alliance, you will need to invest time in building vision and direction – and you will need to keep on doing this, or the energy you have built up will soon dissipate.

Without a vision the people will perish, but when we seek the Kingdom of God together, we can do amazing things!

Questions

1. Can you think of an occasion when a group of people came together to achieve something? How did this happen? What did they achieve?
2. Can you think of an occasion when a group of people failed to achieve something. Why do you think this happened? What could they have done differently?
3. What opportunities do you have to come together with others? What happens at these gatherings? What contributions do you make?
4. What churches or communities exist in your area? What could be done to help them work together more effectively?

7. Action: Faith in Practice

Jesus said to them, "The kings of the Gentiles lord it over them; and those who exercise authority over them call themselves Benefactors. But you are not to be like that. Instead, the greatest among you should be like the youngest, and the one who rules like the one who serves. For who is greater, the one who is at the table or the one who serves? Is it not the one who is at the table? But I am among you as one who serves.

Luke 122.25-27 (NIV)

Organising for Action

The aim of community organising is to help people take action for themselves. It is not enough merely to make a decision, there must be action – and that action should result in a reaction.

This was one of the key principles that Saul Alinsky taught. As he looked at the world of his time, he noticed that people often liked to make a big noise. There were lots of protests and campaigns about things that really mattered. The people who took part in these protests often felt "empowered" but there weren't many concrete results.

Alinsky taught that we need to think about the reaction that we want to achieve and design our actions accordingly. This means having a clear idea about what we want to achieve, and building relationships with people who can actually help us. He had a very pragmatic approach which is worth keeping in mind.

The other key thing about action is that it helps build people up. Much as exercise builds muscles in the body, action builds the strength of a community. Alinsky taught his organisers to look for winnable goals so that communities could gain confidence and capability before moving on to more ambitious projects.

Community organisers often say "action is the oxygen of organising" which means that being involved in a successful action builds up the community, and gives it both the hunger and ability to do more. It is worth noting that action may be the oxygen of organising - but only if you took part in the action... In other words, people grow by being involved. They don't grow if someone else does it for them.

Which brings us to the "Iron Rule" of organising:

Never do for others what they can do for themselves.

I have been an Anglican vicar for over twenty-five years and I have broken this rule every single day.

I remember the first church council meeting that I was asked to chair. I was a young enthusiastic curate who was looking to prove myself. I was a cracking chair! The agenda was carefully crafted, I allowed people to speak, I moved things on, and made sure we came out with some decisions...

It was only afterwards that I realised we had eighteen action points and my name was against every single one!!

There are many reasons why leaders break the iron rule and fall into the D.I.Y. trap.

Many of us choose to do it ourselves because we're convinced that we can do better. We may (or may not) be right, but we miss the opportunity to help someone else to grow.

Some of us are trying to be kind. We think that the job needs doing, but we don't want anyone else to worry about it. Instead, we shift more and more burdens onto ourselves – which means that we don't stop to think or talk it through. We rob other people of the chance to help set priorities.

Many of us just want to avoid conflict. We know that expectations are unrealistic and there might be a better way to do things, but it's easier to go with the flow. This is fair to nobody. It merely increases unrealistic expectations, and creates a cycle of stress, failure and disappointment.

The iron rule of organising is a reminder that the significance of a task is bigger than its output. The classic example is the famous quote from Maimonides:

"Give a man a fish and you feed him for a day;
teach a man to fish and you feed him for a lifetime."

Community organising is not merely a methodology for getting things done, it's also a process for building people up. This means that it's more important to choose actions that help people to learn, develop confidence and work together more effectively. These outcomes are more important than the immediate output of the action itself.

This is why community organisers often focus on small and winnable campaigns before encouraging people to take on big problems. In fact, most people won't believe they can take on the big problems until they've had a few smaller wins. It's like an athlete building up muscle.

Broad-based community alliances are often formed in neglected and disadvantaged areas where people face real problems in their daily lives. Poverty and inadequate housing can be serious issues, but it might be better to begin with smaller (but no less important) problems like road crossings, or women-only swimming sessions. As the alliance gathers momentum, it's possible to move on to bigger things.

The same applies to churches. Many people can feel seriously disempowered by years of being told what they can't do – and ministers who practise D.I.Y. have merely reinforced the feeling that only experts can *do* church. It can take time to build people up so that they feel confident and able to take on significant issues.

The only way to get there is to practise the iron rule.

Small Steps

One of the best campaigns that I have been part of involved children from a primary school. The children of Jubilee Wood Primary School held a listening campaign. They discovered that there was a serious issue with steps on the footpath near to the school. These had been damaged by a lorry a few years ago. They had not been repaired, and had become unsafe over time with exposed metal and crumbling concrete.

The issue of the steps was more significant than the safety issue alone. It suggested that their area – and their school – was not valued. This problem had consequences beyond the physical damage itself.

They collected evidence, listened to stories and took pictures. Tom, our community organiser, arranged for them to meet the leader of the Borough Council. They rehearsed what they were going to say and prepared for their "action".

I met them in the Council offices when they were preparing to go in. They were excited and ready to go. They had photos and hand-drawn posters which explained the problem.

They went in to see the Council Leader who made an immediate commitment to do something about it. Within weeks the problem was sorted.

I think the most exciting thing about this story is that those young people have learned that they are not helpless. Even when everything seemed to be stacked against them, there were things that they could do – and they could be heard by those who hold power. It's important not to underestimate the long-term impact of this one event. "Small steps" can build leaders for the future...

Going Large

Small wins make big wins more likely. When people take up running, they begin with a very short distance - perhaps just as far as the next road junction - but they are soon going much further as their confidence, fitness and enthusiasm increases. The same applies to community organising. Leaders learn through small victories that they can do much more.

The same methodology which enables primary school children to get a few steps fixed, can be scaled up to achieve significant change. Citizens UK is best known for its Living Wage campaign which has had a positive impact on tens of thousands of low paid workers. This began with a local listening exercise in the east end of London.

Small campaigns help leaders to learn the skills that they could use to tackle bigger issues. Most of us feel powerless, but a small win can help build confidence that more is possible.

Going the Distance

The day before writing this paragraph I attended the memorial celebration for Neil Jameson, the founder of Citizens UK. Neil was a giant of community organising, who introduced the idea to the UK following a trip to the states in 1986. Neil spent more than thirty years building chapters and alliances across the UK. He trained and nurtured thousands of leaders and organisers. He achieved some incredible wins, including the end of child detention for asylum seekers, and the introduction of community sponsorship into the UK.

Neil was hugely influential, but I remember him for less visible and public actions...

He was the first in the office in the morning, often unlocking the doors and turning on the lights. He treated everyone with respect and listened to them, whether they were an office cleaner or the prime minister. He didn't just campaign for refugee resettlement, he formed a sponsorship group in his own area to make it happen. He moved chairs, made coffee, listened to everyone and was always ready to help other people with their projects.

The Iron Rule is crucial for organising:

Never do for others what they can do for themselves.

But we are not organisers all of the time. Sometimes we are leaders. Sometimes we are mobilisers or activists. But we are *always* servants, because *we follow a God who serves.*

Neil Jameson set us a powerful example, inspired by his Quaker faith, to use community organising wisely - not as a tool for manipulating or controlling others - but as a way of serving them. We need to remember this in our common life together. It is our small acts of kindness, and our willingness to muck in, that show people how much God loves them.

As Christians we follow Christ who was the ultimate organiser - and the definitive servant. We are called to use the tools at our disposal to build other people up, to set them free, and to seek the Kingdom of God in a broken world.

Questions

1. What makes you angry? What would you like to change?
2. What needs to be done if that change is to happen?
3. Who needs to do something differently or change their mind if that change is to happen?
4. What can you do with others to make this happen?
5. If your answer to question number four is that you haven't got enough power to make this big change happen now, is there something smaller that you could achieve now – which might take you one step towards the bigger goal?
6. Are you willing to do your bit – however small – to achieve big change, or would you rather leave it to others? Think about this carefully. It's the big question...

8. Final Thoughts...

I have been an ordained minister for over twenty-five years. I believed that God was calling me to be a minister so that I could make a difference in the world as a servant of Jesus.

As an Anglican vicar, I did have opportunities to work with people at significant moments in their life – particularly through baptisms, weddings and funerals. These were often deeply moving events and the circumstances were sometimes very difficult. It was good to feel that I had made a difference.

Most of my time as an ordained minister was spent in more mundane work - simply keeping a local Christian community going. I worked long hours, six or seven days a week, trying to keep people happy, and often failing. It was a lot of stress for relatively little gain.

Community organising transformed my ministry. I was now involved in action that had a real impact on people's lives. Instead of spending most of my time with Christians, I was able to work *as a Christian* with a broad range of people beyond the church walls. I watched people grow and change. I learned how to have an impact rather than just make a noise.

I wrote this book because I wanted to pass on some of the lessons that I've learned along the way. It's a small offering which I feel moved to share. I hope it is useful.

One thing I have noted about Citizens UK is that people often focus on the campaigns that have emerged from the alliance: the Real Living Wage, Community Sponsorship, Voter Registration, etc... These are all good projects, but it is equally important to think about the process which led to these campaigns.

Community organising is not really about campaigns, it's about people. It's about real people in real communities, who have real needs. The best community organisers don't lead campaigns, they build up local leaders and help those leaders to work together. They help those leaders to identify the problems that need to be addressed and the solutions which will solve them.

The practice of community organising has a lot to teach those of us who belong to Christian churches. Many of these are lessons from the Gospel that we have forgotten:

The Kingdom of God: Jesus calls us to seek the Kingdom, not to build or maintain churches. We are called to transform ourselves and the world we live in so that it better reflects the will of God. We therefore need to seek healing, justice, reconciliation and peace for all creation. This is a big vision which has implications for us as individuals and as churches.

Relationality: In an age of mass communication, social media and managerialism, it is easy to forget that Jesus focussed his time on individuals in community. Technology is wonderful but it can depersonalise and disconnect us. If we want to achieve deep and genuine change, we need to spend more time with each other. One-to-ones are not a gimmick, but a better way of living.

Results: Most of us like a good moan, and many political campaigns are sadly little more than a group moan. If we really want to achieve something, we need to go deeper and be prepared for a longer journey. I like to remember that **people generally overestimate what can be achieved in three months, but underestimate what can be achieved in three years.** Community organising has taught me how important it is to invest in relationships, alliances, shared goals and detailed plans. All of this takes time, but is essential if you want to see results.

Discipleship: The most significant thing that any of us can do is to build up other people. It is interesting that the first thing that Jesus said to his disciples was that they were to "fish for people" (Matthew 4.19). Our primary task is therefore to help other people find their place in the Kingdom of God. As Christians, we believe that this includes a relationship with God through Christ, but it has other implications. We want people to flourish. We want them to exercise their gifts and fulfil their own calling. We therefore need to think like community organisers who are focused on other people rather than our own achievements.

Jesus: I tried a number of names for this this book before settling on the somewhat provocative title "Christ the Organiser". It turned out to be a very helpful framework. As the project has developed, I have been drawn back again and again to the words and actions of Jesus. Jesus was not a community organiser in the modern sense of the word, but he does have a lot to teach us about how we should organise our communities in the twenty-first century. I have found it really helpful to think about community organising through a Gospel lens. As Christians, we need to keep coming back to Christ as the one who calls.

I would obviously like to think that this book will inspire you as a reader to learn more about community organising . I realise that this is ambitious. You're a busy person and there are lots of other things to think about.

If I can leave you with anything at all, I hope it will be something from this final chapter:

- **Seek the Kingdom of God**
- **Work relationally**
- **Take time to achieve results**
- **Invest in other people**
- **Follow Jesus**

Tim Norwood
Easter 2024

How to have a Great One-to-One

Organising is powered by relationships, and the one-to-one meeting is the most important relational tool we have. People enjoy talking to each other, which is a great start. A good conversation is always fun, but it's worth approaching one-to-ones as a skill which can be developed.

It's important not to be too prescriptive, because things happen in a one-to-one that can't be anticipated. The Spirit blows where it will, so conversations can go in unexpected directions – but it is worth having a plan or a checklist in mind as a framework.

Here is a rough "agenda" for a one-to-one meeting which might help you to refine your practice:

1. **Recognition**
2. **Connection**
3. **Curiosity**
4. **Alignment**
5. **Action**
6. **Commitment**
7. **Evaluation**

8. Follow-up

Things don't always go to plan, but a disciplined approach will often pay off, so let's go through the list in more detail:

1. **Recognition:** Start by saying something about yourself and the other person. You might not have met each other properly before, so it's worth identifying yourself and acknowledging the other person. I usually mention the reason for the meeting. It might be part of a listening campaign or an opportunity to get to know each other better. I might be meeting them because there's an issue one of us wants to talk about, or we might have been introduced through a third-party. Whatever the back story is, it's worth recognising the value of the person you're meeting and letting them know that you are taking them seriously.

2. **Connection:** Small talk is an important stage in any conversation. It's good to begin with subjects that are less threatening and help to build a human connection. The weather is always good (!) or you could ask them about the rest of their day. Sometimes an informal question can generate information that you want to explore further...

3. **Curiosity:** The best one-to-ones involve a lot of deep listening. This is an active process of asking questions that help you to understand what might be really important to the other person.

   Basic human curiosity is a core characteristic of good organisers. The aim is not, however, to delve into the deepest secrets of another person (this is not a therapy session) but to find out more about their public "self-interest": What do they want to achieve? What are they willing to do? What makes them angry?

There may be specific things that you want to know about, but you should expect to learn new things. The other person will have information that you don't so this is an opportunity to benefit from their unique experience and knowledge.

4. **Alignment:** It's natural for people to look for things that they have in common. In a one-to-one, it's normal to move from learning about each other to looking for a common or overlapping agenda.

   This could be the identification of a common cause or project. It might simply be that you can see the value in what the other person is trying to achieve and you want to support them in some way.

5. **Action:** The key question you are working towards is how can you actually help each other? What can you both do to help the other person achieve their goals?

   There are many ways you could help each other. It could involve direct involvement in a project or activity, but new contacts can be equally useful.

   I often ask, "Who do you think I should speak to?" or "Who do you think could help me?"

   If I'm the one providing the new contact, I will usually offer to send an email to smooth the way. This can ensure that something actually happens.

6. **Commitment:** It can be really helpful to finish a one-to-one with a brief summary of what has been said, and a clear statement of the actions that you have both committed to take.

   I find that this helps turn an informal chat into a powerful encounter. It helps to move the conversation from mere observations to guaranteed impact.

7. **Evaluation:** Like every skill, a one-to-one is something that can be improved with practice. The more one-to-ones you have, the better at it you will get – but only if you take time to stop and ask yourself how you might improve.

   You could ask yourself questions like:

   - What went well?
   - What went less well?
   - What could I do better next time?
   - What did I forget to do?
   - What was I hoping to achieve?
   - What did we achieve together?
   - Did we both gain something?

   It's really helpful to do a one-to-one with an observer present so you can discuss it together, or you could ask your conversation partner to evaluate the one-to-one that you've both shared. That can be a strange but really rich discussion!

   Most of the time, you will have to do the evaluation on your own, but it's worth a few minutes of reflection...

8. **Follow-up:** A one-to-one is not a stand-alone event, but a link in a chain. Each conversation is part of a process that is building community and shared power for action. It's therefore important to follow-up the conversation in some way.

   There might be specific actions that you need to take, or you may have promised to introduce people to each other.

   Many organisers make it their practice to write a brief email that summarises the conversation and the actions that you've both agreed. This can be a really helpful reminder both for yourself and the person you have just met. It ensures that the one-to-one is the beginning of something else, rather than an end in itself.

The best one-to-ones feel very natural and fluid, but achieve a great deal. They can be full of surprises and new ideas.

Printed in Great Britain
by Amazon